The Sunday Post, January 3, 1960.

OTHER features of the Sizzling Sixties in brief—

● Huge supplies of oil will come from the Arctic in submarine tankers.

● Colour television.

Twenty-one-inch screens will be replaced by thirty-inch screens.

Trans-Atlantic TV will be possible by relay stations attached to satellites circling the earth.

● In industry the 30-hour week will come in sight

● The Atlantic will be crossed in a few hours by jets with a maximum speed of 2000 miles per hour.

● In athletics seconds will be gradually knocked off the mile record, until it will be run in 3½ minutes.

● On the football pools, it's possible the prize for the treble chance could reach the staggering total of one million pounds for a 2d stake.

● Heated grandstands at football grounds. Pitches free from frost and snow by electrical soil heating

● By 1963, Scotland's new strip mill at Ravenscraig will be producing up to 500,000 tons of steel.

● Scotland will have at least one car factory.

● A heliport in Glasgow by the mid-sixties. Inter-city helicopter services throughout Britain.

YES, it's to be the Sizzling Sixties all right.

The Sunday Post, February 21, 1960. 7

SUNDAY PUBS?—OUR READERS SAY NO

SHOULD the pubs open on Sundays? That's what we asked last week. Now readers have given their verdict. Of the letters we received, 61 per cent. were against opening.

---

12 The Sunday Post, April 17, 1960.

PLEASE KEEP OFF IT, B.B.C.!

ON "Beat The Clock" last Sunday, a couple were presented with a set of four travelling suitcases, a week-end in Paris (Friday to Monday, all expenses paid) and £20 spending money.

On "Pot Luck" the following night, a woman won a set of bathroom scales!

It's no use, B.B.C. If you're not to compete with this giveaway lark in a big way, steer clear of it altogether.

1960

SUNDAY, MAY 8, 1960.

"He Flew 1200 Miles Over Soviet Territory"

"SPY" PILOT CAPTURED —SAYS MR K.

MR KRUSHCHEV said yesterday that Russia had captured "alive and kicking" the pilot of an American plane shot down on May 1.

He said it was shot down more than 1200 miles into Soviet territory on a mission to photograph missile and radar defences.

He identified the pilot as Francis Garry Powers (30), who, he said, was formerly a U.S.A.F. captain, but since 1956 a member of the Central Intelligence Agency.

Wanted—Descendants Of A Tay Bridge Disaster Victim

AN Edinburgh firm of solicitors is trying to trace the relatives of a victim of the Tay Bridge disaster.

The Sunday Post, May 22, 1960.

NOW THROW THE RULE BOOK INTO THE CLYDE!

TODAY, the footballers of Real Madrid are back asking in the sunshine of Spain. With the cheers of Hampden's 127,000 crowd still ringing in their ears.

The players themselves were flabbergasted at the terrific reception they received at the end of Wednesday's European Cup final.

The Sunday Post, June 12, 1960.

18 Towns Could Have Own Radio Stations

LOCAL broadcasting should be the new trend for sound radio.

After ten years on the air, "The Goon Show" came to a close with "The Last Smoking Seagoon". The zany comedy of Milligan, Sellers and Secombe was a huge influence on Peter Cook who, along with Alan Bennet, Jonathan Miller and Dudley Moore created "Beyond the Fringe" which opened at the Edinburgh Festival on 22nd August 1960, launching the "Satire boom" of the 60's, which continued through programmes such as "That Was The Week That Was".

The Sunday Post, July 10, 1960.

RUSSIAN TEDS TRY TO PULL THE KILT OFF THE HON MAN!

SUNDAY, AUGUST 28, 1960.

Fantastic Weather Sweeps Britain

Torrents In North— Tornado In South!

The Sunday Post, October 30, 1960.   7

THE TROGLODYTES

U.S. Forecast That Human Race Will Go Underground

WITHIN three years a lot of us could be living and working deep underground. That is

THE SUNDAY POST, SEPTEMBER 25, 1960.

Has Russia Put A Man In Space?

the Reds lik

SUNDAY, NOVEMBER 6, 1960.

Kennedy Favourite—But Nixon May Sway "Silent Vote"

AMERICAN ELECTION—IT'S A TERRIFIC FINISH!

Stiletto Heel Ban : Some Shops Will Take Back Shoes

SOME Inverness shops have agreed to take back shoes bought by girl pupils of Inverness Royal Academy following a ban by the rector, Dr D. J. Macdonald, on stiletto heels at the annual school dance on December 22.

THE BROONS AND OOR WULLIE – 1960

The Sunday Post 7th February 1960

The Sunday Post 31st January 1960

The Sunday Post 28th February 1960

The Sunday Post 13th March 1960

THE BROONS AND OOR WULLIE – 1960

The Sunday Post 27th March 1960

The Sunday Post 5th June 1960

14

THE BROONS AND OOR WULLIE – 1960

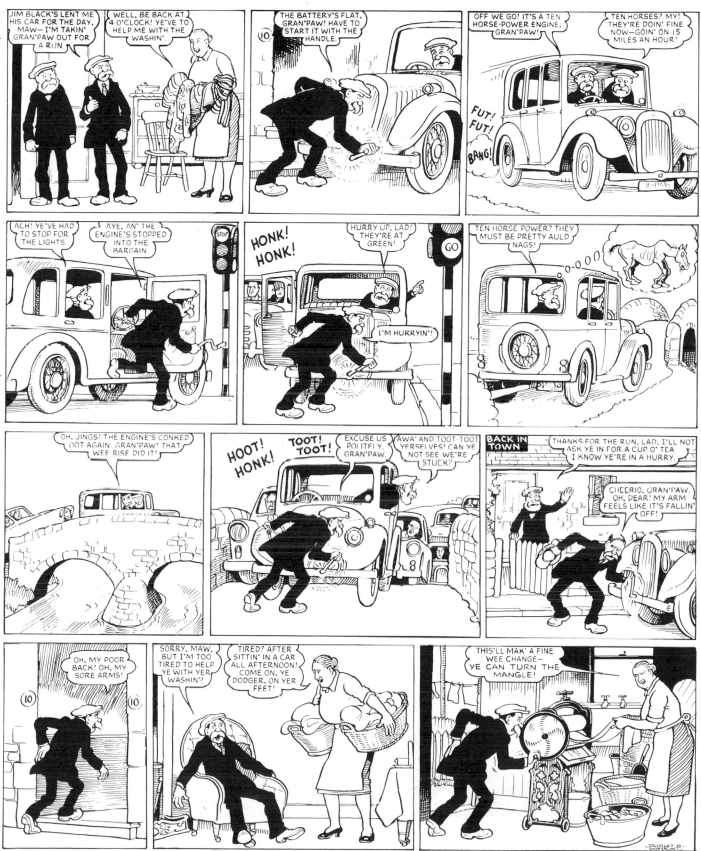

The Sunday Post 16th October 1960

THE BROONS AND OOR WULLIE – 1960

The Sunday Post 6th November 1960

Adapted from the title page of the 1968 Oor Wullie Book.

The Sunday Post, January 22, 1961.

Scots Lose Jobs In Car Slump

SUNDAY, FEBRUARY 19, 1961.

Mac Intervenes Today In Rhodesian Deadlock

"Britain Has Sold Us Down The River" —Africans

1961

The Sunday Post, February 19, 1961.

The Latest—See Marilyn Or Bing While You Fly

Film Shows In Airliners!

The Sunday Post, April 23, 1961.

DALI'S 'LE CHRIST' SLASHED IN GLASGOW ART GALLERY

They're Daft About Jimmy In The Falkland Isles

RECORDS of Jimmy Shand and his band are a big hit in the Falkland Islands, in the South Atlantic. On the...

SUNDAY, SEPTEMBER 3, 1961.

Scotland Yard Men Hear Recordings Of Phone Calls

THREATS TO DESTROY GOYA— AND STEAL MORE PAINTINGS

The Sunday Post, February 19, 1961.

The Sunday Post, May 21, 1961.

Thousands Stage Sit-Down Polaris Protest

CHICO MARX (THE PIANIST) IS CRITICALLY ILL

CHICO MARX, the piano-playing member of the famous Marx Brothers team is critically...

The Sunday Post, April 16, 1961.

"I'D LIKE TO GO TO MARS NOW," SAYS MAJOR YURI

OOR WULLIE TAKES A BOW

IN 1944 Alex. Odendaal was a young submarine wireless operator in the Dutch Navy.

While he was based at Dundee, he was billeted with Mrs Jessie Aird, 40 Perth Road.

Like so many other visitors, he became a keen reader of "The Sunday Post." So much so that since he went back to Holland in 1946, Mrs Aird has sent him the paper every week. She also sends the "Oor Wullie" or "The Broons" Annual at Christmas.

Now Alex.'s family in Nijmegen are daft about "Oor Wullie."

Every week Alex translates his capers into Dutch for Mrs Odendaal and their two children.

Recently the family moved into a new house in Nijmegen. They wanted to give it a name, and they all plumped for OOR WULLIE. The name is set in foot-high letters above the living-room window for all to see.

Oor Wullie himself couldn't be prouder of his name!

The Sunday Post, December 31, 1961.

Major Yuri Gagarin, the first man in space, chats with Prime Minister Harold MacMillan, during a visit to London.

The Sunday Post 29th January 1961

The Sunday Post 22nd January 1961

The Sunday Post 2nd April 1961

THE BROONS AND OOR WULLIE – 1961

The Sunday Post 2nd April 1961

The Sunday Post 16th July 1961

THE BROONS AND OOR WULLIE – 1961

The Sunday Post 30th April 1961

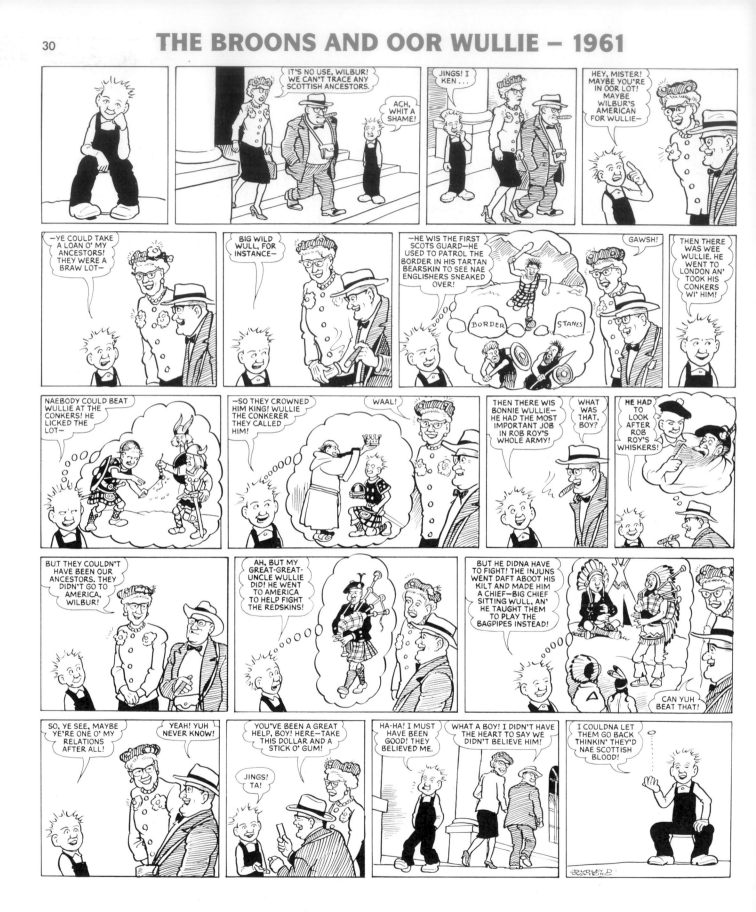

1962

The Sunday Post, January 14, 1962.

1000 In Polaris March – But Not One Arrest

SUNDAY, JANUARY 21, 1962.

Medical Officer's Warning For Bradford

MORE SMALLPOX EXPECTED: VACCINE FLOWN FROM U.S.

The Sunday Post, June 17, 1962.

Regular Trips To The Moon By 1980

SUNDAY, APRIL 8, 1962.

Britain Cuts Down Vital Seconds

NUCLEAR ATTACK: LONGER WARNING

SUNDAY, DECEMBER 30, 1962.

The Sunday Post, October 21, 1962.

"IF BEECHING DOESN'T CHANGE HIS MIND—"

Week-Long Strike Soon— N.U.R. Leader

Ike Books Pipe Band For His Ceilidh At Culzean

The Sunday Post, August 19, 1962.

THERE will be high jinks at the castle tomorrow night when the laird throws his tartan party. For the Castle is Culzean, Ayrshire. And the "laird" is General Eisenhower.
Ike has danged the...

SUNDAY, OCTOBER 28, 1962.

After Kennedy Turns Down Turkey Bases Deal—

CASTRO AGREES TO HALT WORK ON MISSILE SITES

The Sunday Post, December 30, 1962.

BLACK Saturday!

"MATCH OFF"—the words that sum up the sporting picture in Britain yesterday.

From Wick to Watford, snow and ice made it a miserable end to the year's sporting programme—and the outlook for the three-games-in-five-days New Year football fiesta seems pretty bleak.

It was the blackest Saturday in the history of English soccer, with 35 of the 45 League games postponed. Seven Scottish League games were off.

Major football pools, members of the P.P.A., were cancelled.

There was no racing. All Rugby League and most Rugby Union matches were off. Only the electric heating system saved the final Scottish trial at Murrayfield.

Today's Weather

OCCASIONAL snow showers with bright intervals. Wind moderate. Outlook for Monday and Tuesday—Sunny intervals. Periods of sleet or snow in many areas. Extensive frost, especially at night.

This is one of the last photographs of Marilyn Monroe taken in early June 1962, during the filming of "Something's Got To Give".

The Sunday Post 4th February 1962

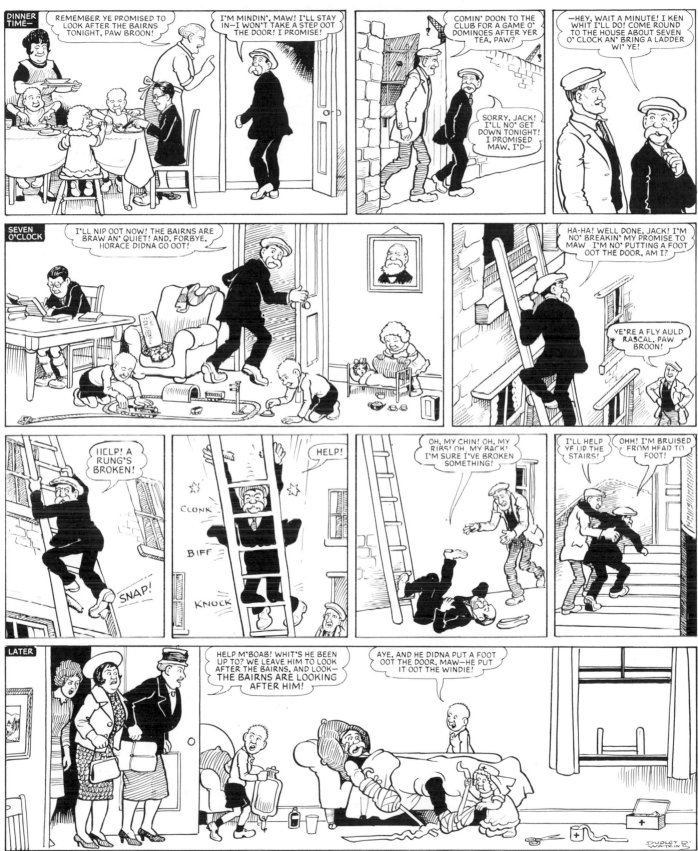

The Sunday Post 19th August 1962

The Sunday Post 26th August 1962

The Sunday Post 15th April 1962

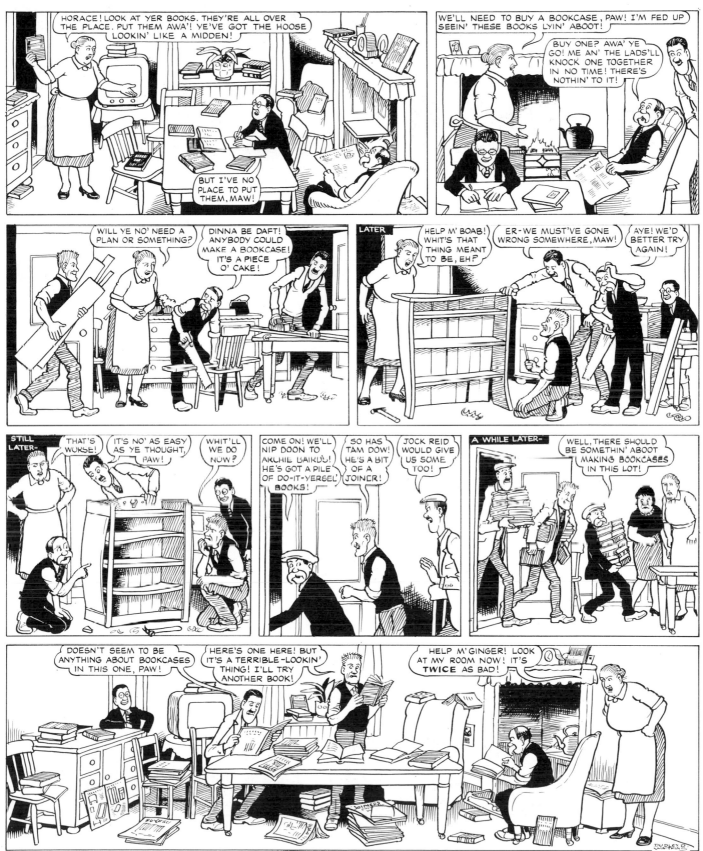

The Sunday Post 9th September 1962

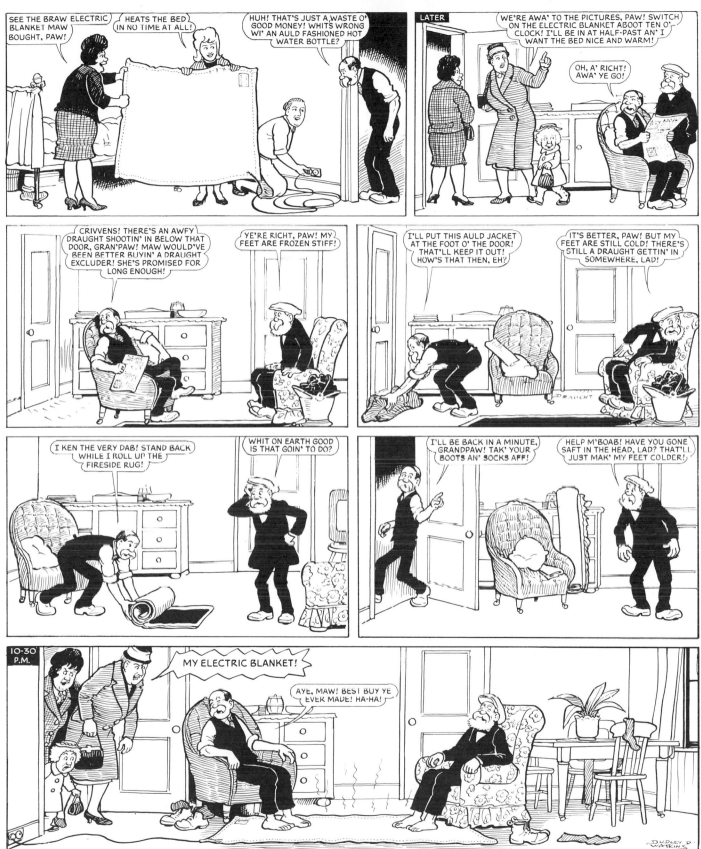

The Sunday Post 9th December 1962

Adapted from the title page of the 1963 Broons Book.

What Do You Say To This, Cassius?

BRILLIANT boxer or boasting big-mouth? That's the question I asked after Cassius Clay's interview on Sportsview.

Bill Crawford, 91 Blackstae Crescent, Pollok, gives his answer in a way that would surely appeal to the heavyweight:—

Oh, Cassius, with your feet of clay,
You've filled us with complete dismay.
You prophesied that in round four
You'd put Doug Jones upon the floor;
Instead of that, with aching joints,
You managed to get home on points.
When next your challenges are flung,
Don't do your fighting with your tongue;
Just make each fist a powered piston—
The tongue's no use with Sonny Liston!

1963

The Sunday Post, June 9, 1963.

END OF THE FREEZE

THE U.S. Weather Bureau predicts the freeze in Britain, Scandinavia and Northern Europe will be broken by rising temperatures this month.

Its 30-day long-range forecast says the cold wave will remain over Southern Europe.

Temperatures in Britain will be "not far below seasonal normal." In parts of Norway they will be above normal.

SUNDAY, MARCH 3, 1963.

PROFUMO: RUMOURS, INNUENDOS AND SUSPICION, SAYS WILSON

SUNDAY, APRIL 21, 1963.

"That Wasn't Part Of Our Programme That Wasn't!"

Bernard Levin Punched In TV Scuffle

The Sunday Post, May 5, 1963.

EX-MARINE CHARGED WITH MURDER OF PRESIDENT

The Sunday Post, November 24, 1963.

"But He Hasn't Confessed"

LEE HARVEY OSWALD (24) was charged with the murder of President Kennedy at Dallas yesterday.

Woman Is Found Stabbed After Twist Party

The Sunday Post, July 28, 1963.

1000 Fans Camp In Street For Beatles Tickets

9000 MORE WILL BE IN QUEUE THIS MORNING

The Sunday Post, October 27, 1963.

The Sunday Post, December 22, 1963.   17

SHEENA'S SKIRT MELTED WHEN SHE SAT AT THE FIRE

B.B.C.-TV

10.30 — LET US WORSHIP GOD. Rev. George Wilkie, Church of Scotland Industrial Organiser.
1.10 — YM MURMUR AFON. The Welsh people and countryside.
1.40 — ANGLICAN AND PRESBYTERIAN.
2.0 — FARMING. Economics of a small farm.
2.30 — CIRCLES OF PANIC. Film, starring Frank Lovejoy.
2.55 — ASSOCIATION FOOTBALL from Hamburg. Germany v. Brazil.
4.45 — NOGGIN AND THE FLYING MACHINE.
4.55 — WAGON TRAIN, starring Polly Bergen.
5.45 — JANE EYRE. Part 5.
6.10 — NEWS.
6.15 — COPING WITH LIFE. Rev. Dr Hugh O. Douglas.
6.45 — SUNDAY STORY continued by David Kossoff.
6.50 — SONGS OF PRAISE from Milford Haven.
7.25 — MEET SAMMY DAVIS, JUN., one of the world's greatest entertainers.
8.10 — PERRY MASON explores new territory when a murderer strikes in a zoo.
9.0 — THE SUNDAY PLAY. Lee Montague, Roy Kinnear in "A Right Crusader." Conflict in the fishing trade at a Northern port.
9.50 — NEWS.
10.0 — THIS NATION TO-MORROW, with Kenneth Allsop.
10.45 — PORTRAIT OF AN OPTIMIST. Talk by Rev. Dr Hugh O. Douglas.

STV

10.0 — SUNDAY SESSION. Adult education hour.
2.15 — FARMING COMMENT.
2.25 — SEEK THE TRUTH. Conscience.
2.55 — INTERNATIONAL FOOTBALL. West Germany v. Brazil.
4.45 — ROVING REPORT.
5.10 — ADVENTURES OF THE SEA HAWK." The Divine Touch."
5.40 — TEMPO, with Portuguese folk singer Amalia Rodrigues.
6.5 — NEWS.
6.15 — SUNDAY BREAK. Young people express their ideas of Church music they'd like to hear.
6.55 — TELEVISION APPEAL. Scottish Mental Health National Appeal.
7.0 — ABOUT RELIGION.
7.25 — NEWS.
7.27 — 77 SUNSET STRIP. Murder takes Jeff Spence to France.
8.25 — PALLADIUM. Kenny Ball, Susan Maughan, Phil Ford, and Mimi Hines, American comedy team.
9.25 — NEWS.
9.35 — DRAMA '63. "The Freewheelers" centres round a group of teenagers who "borrow" cars for kicks.
10.35 — HAWAIIAN EYE. Sea monsters mean trouble for Steele and Lopaka.
11.30 — LATE CALL. Rev. Dr H. C. Thomson, Glasgow.

GRAMPIAN TV

As STV, except for:—
2.30 — EXPEDITION. "Survivors Of The Ice Age."
4.45 — ONCE ABOARD THE

The Beatles on "Ready Steady Go", one of the 60's pop shows.

The Sunday Post 10th March 1963

THE BROONS AND OOR WULLIE – 1963

The Sunday Post 24th February 1963

The Sunday Post 24th March 1963

THE BROONS AND OOR WULLIE – 1963

The Sunday Post 31st March 1963

THE BROONS AND OOR WULLIE – 1963

The Sunday Post 7th April 1963

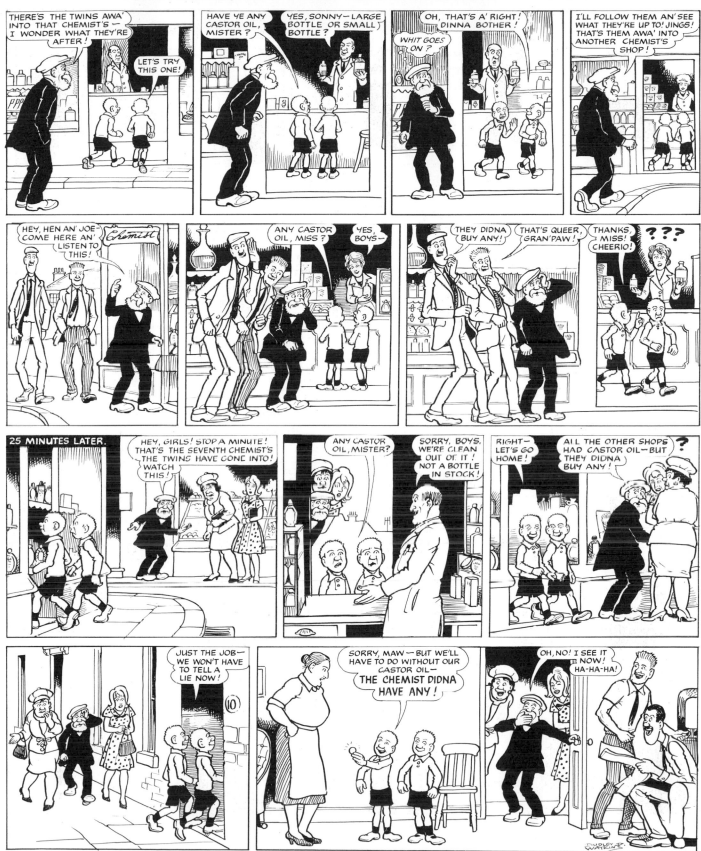

The Sunday Post 28th July 1963

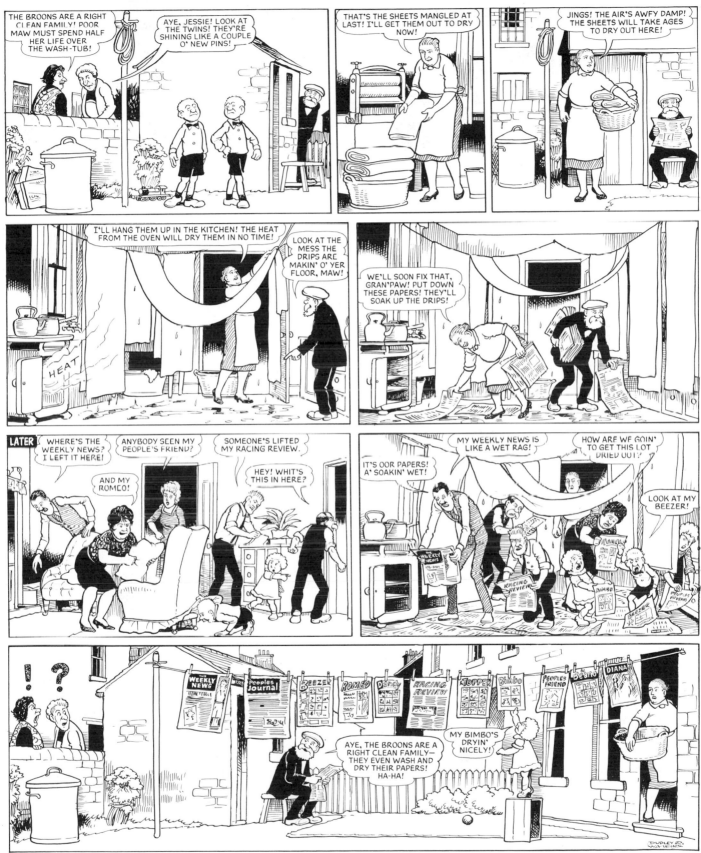

Beatlemania continues unabated.

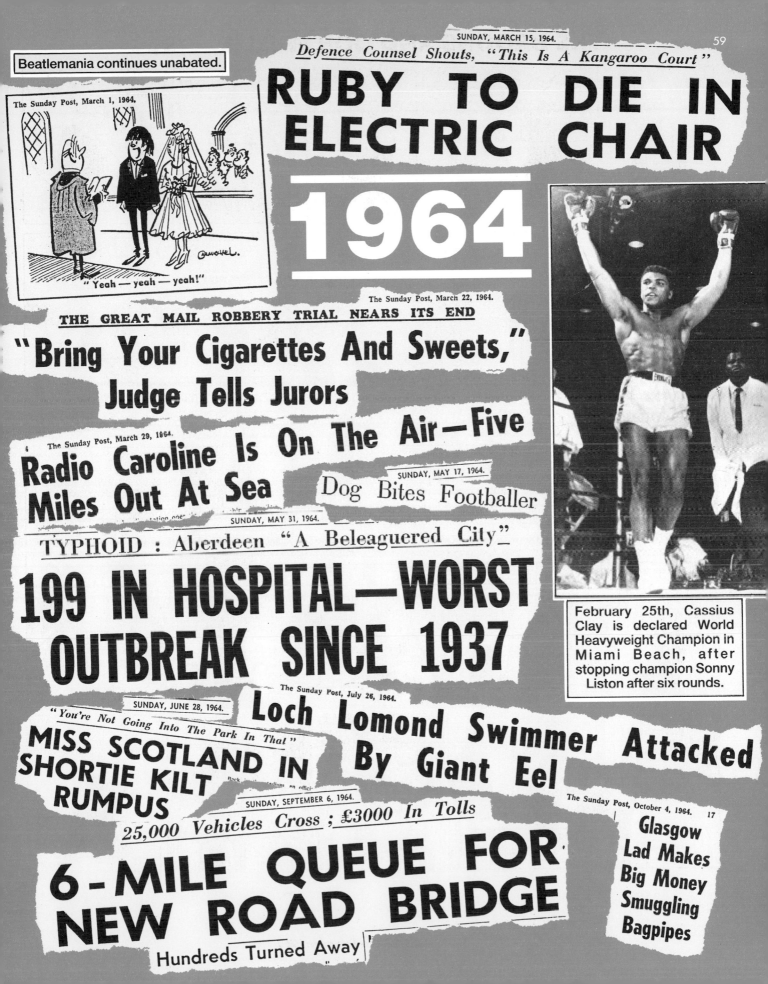

The Sunday Post, March 1, 1964.

"Yeah — yeah — yeah!"

Defence Counsel Shouts, "This Is A Kangaroo Court"

RUBY TO DIE IN ELECTRIC CHAIR

1964

THE GREAT MAIL ROBBERY TRIAL NEARS ITS END

The Sunday Post, March 22, 1964.

"Bring Your Cigarettes And Sweets," Judge Tells Jurors

The Sunday Post, March 29, 1964.

Radio Caroline Is On The Air—Five Miles Out At Sea

SUNDAY, MAY 17, 1964.

Dog Bites Footballer

SUNDAY, MAY 31, 1964.

TYPHOID : Aberdeen "A Beleaguered City"

199 IN HOSPITAL—WORST OUTBREAK SINCE 1937

February 25th, Cassius Clay is declared World Heavyweight Champion in Miami Beach, after stopping champion Sonny Liston after six rounds.

SUNDAY, JUNE 28, 1964.

"You're Not Going Into The Park In That"

MISS SCOTLAND IN SHORTIE KILT RUMPUS

The Sunday Post, July 26, 1964.

Loch Lomond Swimmer Attacked By Giant Eel

SUNDAY, SEPTEMBER 6, 1964.

25,000 Vehicles Cross ; £3000 In Tolls

6-MILE QUEUE FOR NEW ROAD BRIDGE

Hundreds Turned Away

The Sunday Post, October 4, 1964. 17

Glasgow Lad Makes Big Money Smuggling Bagpipes

The Sunday Post 26th April 1964

The Sunday Post 2nd February 1964

The Sunday Post 13th September 1964

The Sunday Post 29th November 1964

The Sunday Post 27th December 1964

Featured here is a unique example* of Dudley Watkins' pencil roughs, found on the back of an inked sheet of Broons artwork which was printed on 2.1.66. An Oor Wullie story similar to the pencilled script had appeared on 29.12.63. We can only speculate that the artist had somehow kept the 1963 script on his desk, and had mistakenly re-drawn it three years later, only for the editorial team to intercept the error at the pencil stage. Whatever happened, it gives a rare insight into the way a page of Watkins artwork was developed.

* (To the knowledge of the current staff.)

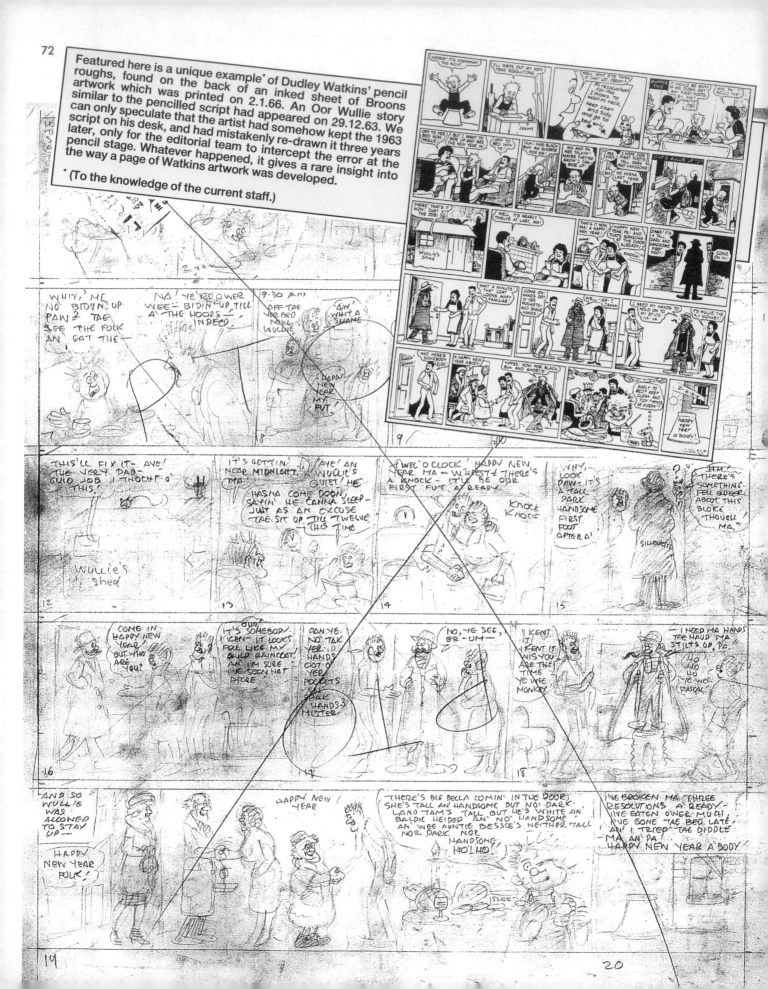

SUNDAY, JANUARY 3, 1965.

"THIRD MAN" PHILBY SAYS RUSSIA IS MARVELLOUS

First Time Seen Since Vanishing

The Sunday Post, January 24, 1965.

They Ate Their Coats To Stay Alive!

FOUR lumberjacks, left without food in a Siberian forest for 10 days, ate their sheepskin jackets to keep alive, the newspaper "Soviet Russia" reported yesterday.

They fried them and found them easier to chew.

The newspaper said the leader of the road-making expedition apparently forgot he had sent the four men to the forest.

1965

SUNDAY, AUGUST 1, 1965.

Flying Saucer Woke Them Up!

HOWLING dogs woke up the McClintock family at Goonumbla, New South Wales, early yesterday.

The family said they rushed out of their farmhouse to see a flying saucer hovering over the farmyard.

The "saucer" had three rods protruding, one from the top and two from the bottom. It was emitting two beams of light.

The "saucer" hovered for about 15 minutes before moving off. Then two of the McClintock boys, aged 12 and 10, admitted they had seen it th day before but had kept it secret.

The incident was reported only five miles away from a big radio telescope.

SUNDAY, JANUARY 31, 1965.

QUEEN LEADS THE NATION'S HOMAGE

WINSTON SPENCER CHURCHILL, the man who made history, passed into its pages yesterday.

Big Viet Cong Attack As U.S. Marines Land

The Sunday Post, April 11, 1965.

SUNDAY, MARCH 21, 1965.

FARMERS THREATEN MEATLESS MONTH

Outcry Over Prices Review

The Sunday Post, August 1, 1965.

Who Threw Dye Into Portobello Pool?

SOUTH AFRICA 'NATIONAL CANCELLED

SUNDAY, SEPTEMBER 12, 1965.

Airport Riots As The Rolling Stones Fly In

SUNDAY, JULY 11, 1965.

HUNT FOR BIGGS: POLICE IN SECOND SWOOP

A new fashion item makes its first appearances. The mini-skirt has arrived.

The Sunday Post 3rd January 1965

The Sunday Post 24th January 1965

The Sunday Post 31st January 1965

THE BROONS AND OOR WULLIE – 1965

The Sunday Post 9th May 1965

The Sunday Post 21st February 1965

Adapted from the title page of the 1964 Oor Wullie Book.

The Sunday Post, January 23, 1966. 3

No Honeymoon Yet For A
Beatle And
His Bride

NEWLYWEDS Beatle George Harrison and his bride, model Pattie Boyd, went to London yesterday to meet the world's press. Surrounded by cameras and reporters George said, " It's...

1966

SUNDAY, MARCH 20, 1966.

Man From U.N.C.L.E. On Mealie Pudding Trail!

ILLYA KURYAKIN (actor David McCallum) flew home to Glasgow yesterday in hush-hush " Man From U.N.C.L.E." style.

The Sunday Post, February 6, 1966. 19

Hundreds Of Dogs And Cats Are Down With Flu

SUNDAY, APRIL 3, 1966.

BLIZZARD TRAPS HAMPDEN FANS

U.S. Space Scientist Joins Scots Buddhist Hideout

The Sunday Post, July 24, 1966. 3

SUNDAY, JULY 31, 1966.

LONDON'S NIGHT OF REJOICING

Amazing Scenes To Celebrate Cup Triumph

WHAT a night it was for London! The scenes to celebrate England's World Cup win were reminiscent of the end-of-the-war jubilation.

SUNDAY, AUGUST 21, 1966.

Five Say They Saw "Nessie"

THE AGONY OF ABERFAN

SUNDAY, OCTOBER 23, 1966.

Bobby Moore, the captain of England, receives the Jules Rimet Trophy from the Queen.

SUNDAY, OCTOBER 23, 1966.

MASTER SPY ESCAPES

GEORGE BLAKE, who is serving a 42-year sentence for spying for Russia, escaped from Wormwood Scrubs last night.

SUNDAY, DECEMBER 11, 1966.

DEFIANT RHODESIA ACCUSES BRITAIN

Wilson's "Dire Warnings" During Tiger Talks

SUNDAY, DECEMBER 18, 1966.

FLOODS TERROR IN NORTH SCOTLAND

The Sunday Post 23rd January 1966

The Sunday Post 27th February 1966

The Sunday Post 30th January 1966

The Sunday Post 13th March 1966

The Sunday Post 20th February 1966

The Sunday Post 10th July 1966

The Sunday Post 26th June 1966

The Sunday Post 14th August 1966

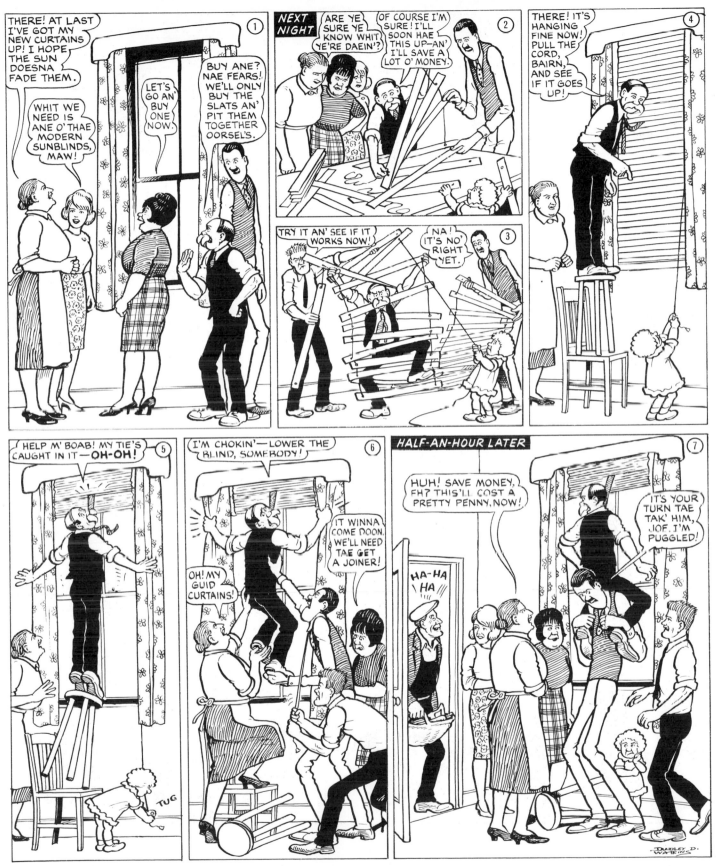

The Sunday Post 24th July 1966

THE BROONS

Adapted from the title page of the 1961 Broons Book.

1967

Baby Boy Born 2000 Ft Above Glasgow

APRIL 16, 1967.

JUBILANT SCOTS TAKE WEMBLEY TURF HOME!

The Sunday Post, March 26, 1967.

Army To Take Full Control Of Aden

THIRTY THOUSAND Scots football fans t wild at Wembley erday after their team beaten England's rld champions 3-2 in an ion - packed interna-nal.

The Sunday Post, May 28, 1967.

The Night Celts Put Us Back On The Map

Two great Scottish football victories, the first at Wembley and the second in Lisbon.

unday Post, September 17, 1967.

Q4 GETS ET FOR BIG DAY

Q4 was the official name of the liner QE2, the real name being a closely guarded secret up until its launch.

The Sunday Post, August 13, 1967.

POP PIRATES—THE LAST DISC TOMORROW

The Sunday Post, October 29, 196;

POLICE ARMED AFTER THREE LIONS ESCAPE

The Sunday Post, December 3, 1967.

What You Want To Know About Coloured TV

LAST night colour TV was officially switched on in Scotland.

Sunday Post, November 26, 1967

Staggering List Of Price Increases On The Way

SUNDAY, DECEMBER 31, 1967.

"No Heart Condition Hopeless Any More," Says Transplant Surgeon

The Sunday Post 26th February 1967

The Sunday Post 5th February 1967

THE BROONS AND OOR WULLIE – 1967

The Sunday Post 9th July 1967

The Sunday Post 30th July 1967

The Sunday Post 20th August 1967

The Sunday Post 8th October 1967

1968

The Sunday Post, February 11, 1968.

Helicopter Rescue For 500 Starving Sheep

The Sunday Post, March 24, 1968.

POLICE BATTLE WITH 3000 HIPPIES

SUNDAY, JUNE 9, 1968.

LUTHER KING: MAN HELD IN LONDON

Extradition On Murder Charge Move

JAMES EARL RAY — wanted in connection with the murder of Martin Luther King—was arrested in London yesterday.

The Sunday Post, October 13, 1968.

Worst Year Ever For Wasps

HOSPITALS up and down the country have treated hundreds of men, women and children this summer for wasp stings.

SUNDAY, AUGUST 25, 1968.

WHERE IS DUBCEK? —MYSTERY DEEPENS

SUNDAY, DECEMBER 29, 1968.

LULU TO WED BEE GEE

In Moscow, Say Czechs: In Prague, Say Russians

THE mystery deepened last night of the whereabouts of Mr Alexander Dubcek, the Czech reformist leader.

The Sunday Post, April 14, 1968.

Bank Gives Out Decimal Coins

A BIRMINGHAM bank jumped the decimal gun yesterday and issued £10 worth of five new pence coins.

The Sunday Post, June 9, 1968.

How Surgeons Fought To Save Bobby Kennedy

President Dubcek's reforms known as "The Prague Spring", lead Russia to send military force into Czechoslovakia.

SUNDAY, OCTOBER 13, 1968.

RHODESIAN TALKS— GAP IS ENORMOUS

The Sunday Post 10th March 1968

The Sunday Post 7th January 1968

THE BROONS AND OOR WULLIE – 1968

THE BROONS AND OOR WULLIE – 1968

The Sunday Post 28th April 1968

THE BROONS AND OOR WULLIE – 1968

The Sunday Post 7th July 1968

THE BROONS AND OOR WULLIE – 1968

The Sunday Post 14th July 1968

Adapted from the title page of the 1967 Broons Book.

The Sunday Post, February 2, 1969.

Hunt For Biggs Stepped Up

RONALD BIGGS, the

SUNDAY, JULY 13, 1969.

JACKLIN MAKES IT A BRITISH OPEN

"Greatest Moment Of My Life"

1969

SUNDAY, FEBRUARY 16, 1969.

Deported For Wearing Mini-Skirt

SUNDAY, JULY 6, 1969.

Hyde Park Jam-Out: Stones' Tribute To Brian Jones

ABOUT a quarter of a million fans at a concert in Hyde Park yesterday heard the Rolling Stones pay tribute to Brian Jones.

Jones was found dead in the swimming pool of his home last week.

Marianne Won't Marry Jagger

MISS MARIANNE FAITHFULL 22-year-old actress frie...

SUNDAY, JULY 20, 1969.

APOLLO 11 IN ORBIT ROUND THE MOON

Ready For Landing Tonight

The Sunday Post, August 24, 1969.

Council Cracks Down On A Badger

50,000 Dylan Fans Camp Out On "Pop" Island

THE great trek to the Isle of Wight gathered momentum yeste...

The Sunday Post, August 31, 1969.

SUNDAY, OCTOBER 19, 1969.

Stolen Tatties Could Be Deadly

The Sunday Post, October 5, 1969.

A New Pack Of Jokers Tonight!

Apollo 11, crewed by Neil Armstrong, Edward "Buzz" Aldrin and Michael Collins, successfully places a lunar module on the moon's surface.

B.B.C. are making a bold bid tonight to break ITV's hold on late Sunday-night audiences.

The four Davids — Frost, Allen, Jacobs and Nixon — have had things all their own way until now. B.B.C. have considered similar shows, but have taken the plunge and finally decided to concentrate on comedy.

They're pinning their hopes on Monty Python's Flying Circus, a 30-minute nutty comedy series. They've been working for six months on it.

Four of the stars, who are also writing the series, are well established in comedy. John Cleese was a deadpan comic in The Frost Report. Graham Chapman, Terry Jones and Michael Palin all wrote sketches for the last Marty Feldman series.

Watch for clever animated sketches by artist Terry Gilliam. He takes Old Masters and brings them to life.

It sounds good. About eleven o'clock tonight you'll be able to judge for yourself.

John Cleese.

The Sunday Post, September 14, 1969.

King-Size Kippers Mystery

The Sunday Post 12th January 1969

The Sunday Post 2nd March 1969

The Sunday Post 9th March 1969

The Sunday Post 9th February 1969

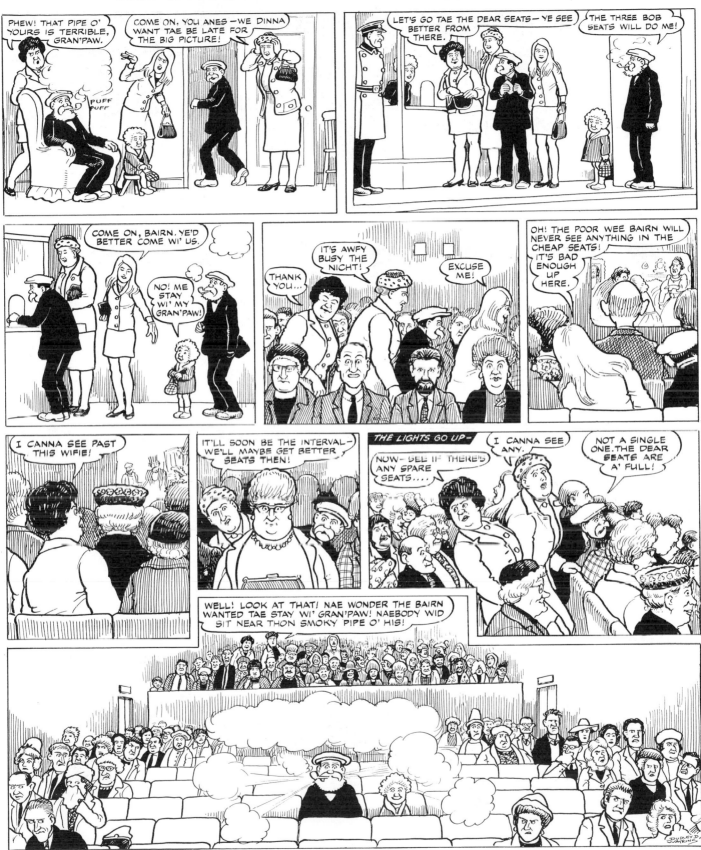

The Sunday Post 24th August 1969

DUDLEY DEXTER WATKINS

Wullie's first appearance March 1936

Oor Wullie, as the 60's draw to a close

In 1907, Dudley Dexter Watkins was born in Nottingham. From an early age he showed an aptitude for illustration. He attended the Nottingham School of Art, and in 1925 he moved to Dundee to work for D. C. Thomson and Co. Ltd., where he would go on to draw an astonishing range of adventure and cartoon pages.

In 1936 he illustrated The Broons and Oor Wullie for The Sunday Post's newly conceived Fun Section.

The strips are regarded as classics of their kind. On August 20th, 1969, he died suddenly at his desk.

He had drawn close to three and a half thousand Broons and Oor Wullie pages.

The Broons' debut March 1936

The Broons 1969 style

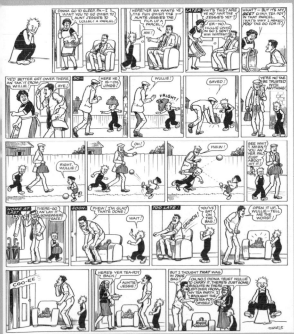

ISBN 0-85116-712-8